Dedicated To:
Gavin & Corbin

ritten By: Abigail Gartland

That is a hard name to say. Let's practice!

AW-GUS-TEEN

Great job!

When I was young, I lived with my family. You might know my mom, St. Monica!

I was born in Africa in the 400s.

When I was young, I wanted to do anything I pleased.

I spent my life doing whatever I wanted and making very bad choices.

I had a friend who joined me in breaking rules and doing bad things. God spoke to my friend!

God told him that he was a living in a way that kept him far away from God. My friend was overcome with sadness for his sins.

My friend stopped making bad choices and started living for God. He became an example to me of how I should live, too.

I prayed to God to ask Him for His help. My mom also prayed a lot for me.

I became close to God, and a few years later, I became a priest.

I spent the rest of my life spreading the word of God!

Do you want to be more like me?

You can celebrate my feast day with me on August 28th.

I am the patron saint of sinners.

I pray for you every day of your life.

St. Augustine, Pray for us!

Copyright:

Clipart:  © PentoolPixie   © LimeandKiwiDesigns
Licensed purchased: 1/10/2024

About the Author

Abigail Gartland

I love the saints and I love my faith. The idea for sharing the stories of the saints with little ones came when my dear friends were expecting their first baby. I wanted to create something as unique and special as our friendship. Each book is dedicated to very special people and groups who have enriched my faith in different ways. I am blessed to write these stories and appreciate the unending support of my family and friends. When I am not writing, I am a middle school teacher. I hope you enjoy these stories. I pray for each and every person who opens one of my books to learn more about the saints.

Abbie

www.ingramcontent.com/pod-product-compliance
Lightning Source LLC
LaVergne TN
LVHW061633070526
838199LV00071B/6663